Vocal Workouts for the Contemporary Singer

Anne Peckham

Berklee Media

Vice President: Dave Kusek
Dean of Continuing Education: Debbie Cavalier
Director of Business Affairs: Robert Green
Associate Director of Technology: Mike Serio
Marketing Manager, Berkleemusic: Barry Kelly
Senior Graphic Designer: Robert Heath

Berklee Press

Senior Writer/Editor: Jonathan Feist
Production Manager: Shawn Girsberger
Marketing Manager, Berklee Press: Jennifer D'Angora

Special thanks to April Thomas, Meghan C. Joyce, Chandra Cogburn, and Chris Bilton for editorial and production support.

Library of Congress Cataloging-in-Publication Data

Peckham, Anne.
  Vocal workouts for the contemporary singer / Anne Peckham.
      p. cm.
  ISBN 0-87639-047-5 (978-0-87639-047-4)
  1. Singing–Instruction and study. I. Title.

  MT820.P33 2006
  783'.043–dc22

                                2005019007

Printed in the United States of America by Vicks Lithographic and Printing Co., Inc.

12 11 10 09 08 07 06 05   6 5 4 3 2 1

1140 Boylston Street
Boston, MA 02215-3693 USA
(617) 747-2146
Visit Berklee Press Online at
www.berkleepress.com

DISTRIBUTED BY

HAL•LEONARD®
CORPORATION
7777 W. BLUEMOUND RD. P.O. BOX 13819
MILWAUKEE, WISCONSIN 53213

Visit Hal Leonard Online at
www.halleonard.com

Contents

CD Tracks

Track

Acknowledgments

SPECIAL THANKS TO Adriana Balic, Debbie Cavalier, Jonathan Feist, Peter Kontrimas, Susan Gedutis Lindsay, Matt Marvuglio, Rick Peckham, Lisa Thorson, and Jan Shapiro.

CD Credits

Piano:	Mark Shilansky (www.markshilansky.com)
Bass:	Bruno Råberg (www.brunoraberg.com)
Drums:	Take Toriyama
Guitar:	Rick Peckham (www.rickpeckham.com)
Vocals:	Robin McKelle (www.robinmckelle.com)
	Paul Pampinella (Five O'Clock Shadow: www.focs.com; Vox One: www.voxone.net)
	Anne Peckham (www.annepeckham.com)
	Jeff Ramsay

THIS BOOK IS FOR SINGERS who are interested in contemporary, non-classical singing styles. It is a look at breath support, tone production, and voice strengthening, plus material for more experienced singers who want to continue to develop their voices. By following the Complete Vocal Workouts presented here, you will be able to sing with improved range, agility, sound, and overall expressive power.

In part I, you will find a review of the basics to help anchor your technique with renewed awareness of healthy singing. Some of these topics, and many others, are covered in greater depth in the companion book, *The Contemporary Singer* (Berklee Press, 2000).

The Complete Vocal Workouts in part II form the heart of this volume. These exercises will help you warm up your voice before you sing, as well as develop your range, agility, stamina, and other aspects of your instrument. Each vocal exercise is written out so you can follow along with the music as you sing. You can isolate specific exercises, or follow through the entire CD workout. If you don't read music, you can just use your ear, and learn the exercises from the CD, though scanning the notation for lyrics may be a help to you. Icons show the complete range of each exercise in the book, from the highest to the lowest note. When the exercises in the Advanced Workout divide into low and high voice versions, both ranges are indicated. This will help you determine whether the high- or low-voice workout is best for you.

You will find a variety of fun and challenging vocal workouts that will stimulate your creative side while you refine your voice. You will also see Two- and Three-Part Exercises. In these, you can sing in harmony along with other voices on the CD. You will learn to tune your voice to other singers, just as you would when performing background vocals. It's fun to sing with other voices, and these exercises will help you develop valuable skills needed by all singers.

The following chart suggests several practice routines. Choose whichever one best fits your vocal needs and your schedule.

COMPLETE VOCAL WORKOUTS

Timings

Warm-ups:	12 minutes
Basic Vocal Workout :	15 minutes
Advanced Vocal Workout:	12 minutes
Singing Harmony: Two- and Three-Part Exercises:	8 minutes
Cool Down:	5 minutes (Tracks 2 and 3, repeated from Warm-ups)

Always sing the Warm-ups for All Voices before singing the Basic, Advanced, or Part Exercises. Choose either the high- or low-voice version of the Basic and Advanced Workout for the suggested routines below. Repeat tracks 2 and 3 to cool down after singing.

Suggested Vocal Workout Routines

Complete Basic Vocal Workout (32 minutes)

Warm-ups + Basic Vocal Workout (choose high or low voice) + Cool Down = 32 minutes

Complete Advanced Workout (29 minutes)

Warm-ups + Advanced Vocal Workout (choose high or low voice) + Cool Down = 29 minutes

Advanced Extended Vocal Workout (44 minutes)

Warm-ups + Basic Vocal Workout + Advanced Vocal Workout + Cool Down = 44 minutes

Part Singing Vocal Workout (40 minutes)

Warm-ups + Basic Vocal Workout + Two- and Three-Part Exercises + Cool Down = 40 minutes

Advanced Extended Vocal Workout with Parts Exercises (52 minutes)

Warm-ups + Basic Vocal Workout + Advanced Vocal Workout + Two- and Three-Part Exercises + Cool Down = 52 minutes

HEALTHY SINGING RANGES

If the highest notes in the vocal exercises on this CD are out of your range, be sure you're not forcing your lower register up beyond your comfort zone. Try to release into a lighter head-voice tone to sing higher notes, instead of pushing. Work to make these transitions as smooth as possible. Lighten up just before the switch when going upward, and keep your tone light as you descend in pitch. Read chapter 4 for more information on vocal registers.

- Getting Ready to Sing

- Breathing

- The Four P's

- Vibrato, Vocal Registers, and Belting

- Essential Vocal Care

- Auditioning

PART I

VOCAL ESSENTIALS

THERE ARE TWO BASIC TYPES OF VOCAL EXERCISES included in part II's workouts: warm-ups and voice builders.

Warm-ups will gradually prepare your muscles for the higher intensity of performance. They will help re-establish efficient breathing technique and bring your attention to the body/mind connection in singing. Warm-ups will also help you sing high notes more easily. The best types of vocal warm-up exercises are descending slides, lip or tongue trills, scales with changing vowels, and staccato arpeggios.

The voice-building exercises you will find here are stylistically diverse and can be helpful and fun for singers of rock, pop, jazz, and r&b music. You can gain all the benefits of regular practice, keeping your voice in shape, building new skills, and learning new patterns and riffs for improvising. You can also develop a good vocal sound, build strength and stamina, and build rhythmic, tonal, and pitch skills. You will do all this while using sounds and patterns that are stylistically appropriate to your idiom. Depending on your vocal needs, the best voice-building exercises may consist of long tones, pentatonic arpeggios, intervallic leaps, and scales or other patterns covering an octave or more in range on various vowel sounds. In these workouts, you will encounter all of these types of voice builders. The long-tone exercise below is another example of an effective voice builder.

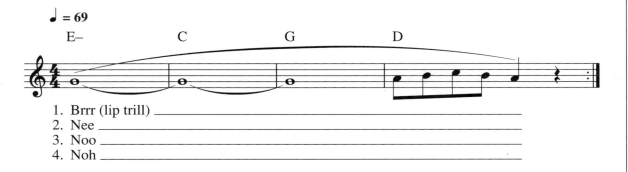

1. Brrr (lip trill) _____
2. Nee _____
3. Noo _____
4. Noh _____

PRACTICING WITH THE VOCAL WORKOUTS CD

Regular practice will help you to improve your voice and to maintain your sound. The Vocal Workout CD makes it easy to stay focused. Just sing the Warm-up for All Voices, then choose one of the Complete Vocal Workouts on the CD, and sing along. (See the introduction, page ix, for suggested practice routines.) A variety of styles are used to make the workouts fun and to develop skills that you'll need to sing contemporary music.

When you are working with the practice CD, you will need a quiet room with a mirror and a CD player. Although you can sing along with the CD without a keyboard or guitar, an instrument can be helpful to check your range to see how high and low you are singing. Stand in front of the mirror while singing to check your posture and to see any signs of physical strain. Sing standing up, to maximize your breath capacity and to minimize any tension in your neck, shoulders, and chest.

GETTING YOUR VOICE INTO SHAPE

If you haven't maintained a consistent training regimen for a period of time, or if you are a beginner, you will need to gradually build your voice.

To initiate your training, or to recondition your voice, start by practicing twenty minutes a day, three to four times a week. Over a period of several weeks, build up to practicing four to six times a week for up to forty-five minutes. Most of the benefits of any previous training are totally lost after four to eight weeks of vocal inactivity, so you will probably feel that you are starting from scratch, if you haven't sung in a while. Vocalizing two days a week or less will probably not improve your singing, if you're out of shape. On the other hand, vocalizing intensively for an hour or more, for six or seven days a week, increases the risk of overuse injury and does not improve vocal condition. Find a balance in your routine that challenges you but allows for some down time.

If you are an experienced singer working to maintain or further develop your vocal sound, it usually isn't difficult to practice four to six times a week for thirty to forty-five minutes. Again, use common sense about the frequency of practice. Pay attention to the way you feel, and consult a vocal technique teacher experienced in working with contemporary music singers if you have any questions about your voice. *This book is not meant to replace professional, private vocal instruction.*

LISTENING TO YOUR BODY

If you feel tired after you sing, check to be sure you aren't forcing your voice or straining. Pay attention to how your voice feels during and after practice. Although you might feel some initial tiredness from using muscles that you've never exercised before, this should subside in a couple of hours after practicing. Your voice will become stronger as you continue to practice.

Exercising new muscles might make you feel a little tired at first, but this is very different from the feeling of vocal strain. You will recover relatively quickly from fatigue caused by exercising new muscles. Fatigue caused by improper singing technique requires much more recovery time.

Normal muscle fatigue caused by exercising your voice usually subsides in one to two hours. Fatigue caused by vocal strain can last a day or more. Discomfort from infection or virus can take a week to ten days to heal. Although viruses can temporarily keep you from singing, you can help yourself by drinking lots of fluids and resting. If you have an infection, you must receive medical attention.

If you practice for a sensible amount of time and end up with a raspy voice, consider other possible causes.

- Are you coming down with a cold?
- Did you sleep in a room with dry air?
- Are you drinking enough water?
- Do you drink more than two cups of coffee each day?
- Did you consume a large, rich, or spicy meal just before bedtime and then wake up hoarse?
- A woman's monthly cycle can make her voice sluggish and unusually low or heavy.
- Are you singing too hard or pushing your voice?

Pay attention to your voice and body, and weigh all possible factors. If you are unsure of the cause of hoarseness, and if it is persistent, consult a voice specialist (laryngologist) to help you identify a course of action that will help you get better.

If you're out of practice, gentle, regular exercises will help progress your singing and develop the kind of coordination your vocal muscles need. Harsh, rough vocal work can overtax your voice and might lead to permanent damage. You don't need "weight lifting" strength for singing. You need light, flexible, coordinated movement of your vocal muscles and balanced breath support. This can be developed with the right kind of practice.

There is no doubt that certain kinds of music are harder on the voice than others. For example, hard rock or heavy metal is a higher-risk style of singing that can wear out your voice faster than most jazz singing. But all kinds of music can put your voice at risk if you don't know what you're doing, especially if you don't warm up before singing.

If you keep your body in good condition and your technique up-to-date, you can head off any problems before serious damage occurs. This requires a heightened sense of self-awareness. You have to know your voice, your requirements for healthy living, your limitations, and when to give your voice a rest. A lot of vocal problems can be prevented with some basic common sense and with devotion to a healthy lifestyle.

Chapter 2. Breathing

SINGERS TYPICALLY LEARN BREATHING TECHNIQUE in their first voice lessons. The idea of low-body, diaphragmatic breathing is not a complicated concept. But remember: *breath support takes minutes to learn and a lifetime to master.* Understanding this concept intellectually does not mean that your muscles will automatically respond when you sing. You must consistently practice good breathing technique until it becomes second nature. This is why many professional performers check in with their voice teachers regularly to make sure their voices are functioning well, and put into place any corrective measures necessary to ensure efficient production that minimizes strain.

The usual in and out of airflow is fine for everyday activities, but efficient management of your breath can give you better vocal control, make your voice freer and more powerful, and give you better stamina.

Even if you already know how to breathe properly for singing, spend a few minutes at each practice session refreshing your skills. When you reinforce proper breath management at the beginning of each practice, you'll be more likely to continue that action for extended periods of singing. This creates a better foundation for all styles of singing.

> ## THE FOUR STEPS OF EFFECTIVE BREATHING
>
> 1. Align your body with neutral posture (described below).
> 2. Inhale, expanding around your waistline.
> 3. Exhale with firm abdominals.
> 4. Keep your ribs open as you exhale. Don't collapse your chest.

NEUTRAL POSTURE

The stresses of carrying bags, books, sitting at a computer for long periods of time, and other bad postural habits can pull your body out of alignment, causing tension, shoulder and back pain, and even muscle spasms. Proper alignment, or keeping a "neutral" spine, places the least stress on your muscles because you are balancing the effort among all your muscles to maintain your position.

To check for neutral posture, try out these various postural extremes. The postural extremes described on the following pages are a method of finding your best body position. By stretching to extreme postures, such as an over-extended chest position, you can get a better idea of what neutral posture feels like as you release the stretch.

Establishing neutral posture

1. Stand with feet hip-width apart.

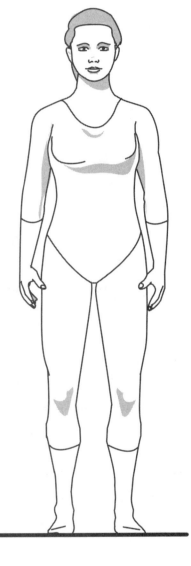

2. Bend your knees into a semi-squat, then straighten your legs, keeping your knees "soft," not locked.

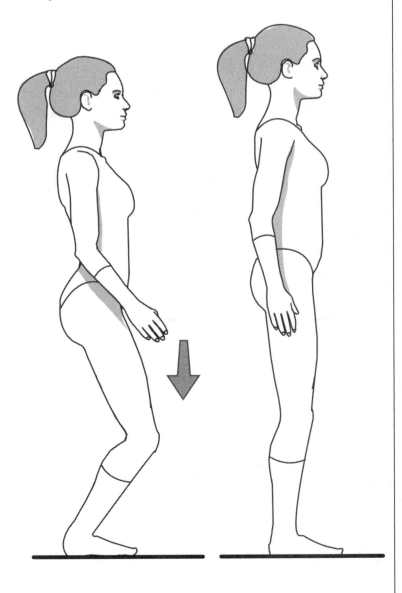

3. Exhaling, squeeze your buttocks together and pull in your stomach muscles, making your lower back very flat. Then, relax your muscles so that your pelvis tips back slightly. Be sure that you are not arching your lower back.

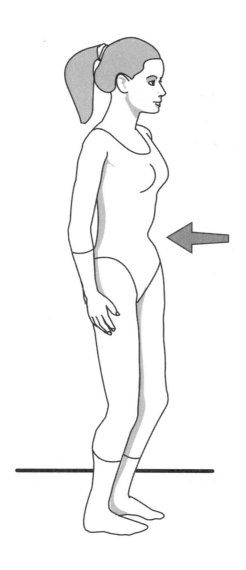 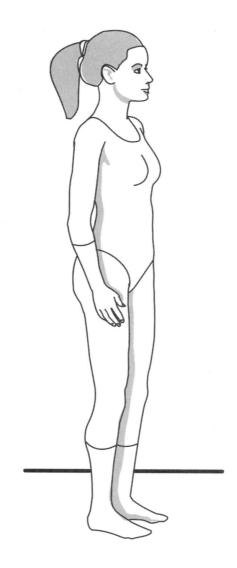

4. Arch your upper back, extending your chest forward, and gently pressing your elbows behind you and your shoulders back. Then release the extended position, maintaining a comfortably high chest position.

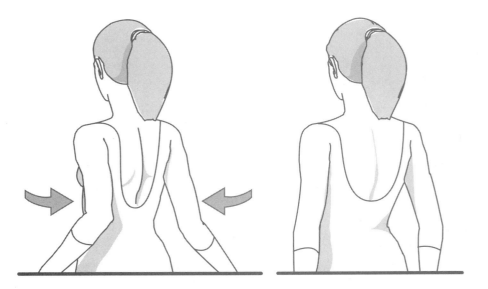

5. Lift your shoulders toward your ears, then drop them, letting your shoulders hang loosely.

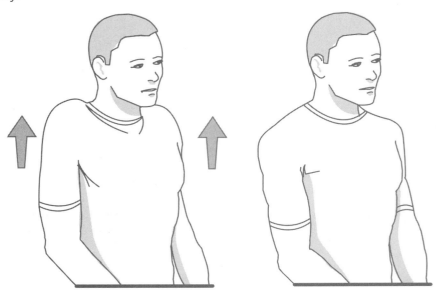

6. Elongate your spine, feeling as if you're lifting the top of your head to the ceiling. Relax a little, maintaining the feeling of spinal lift.

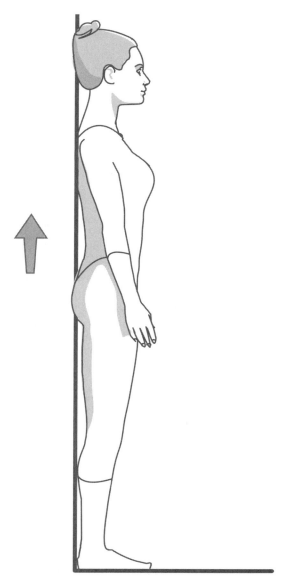

Spine stretched

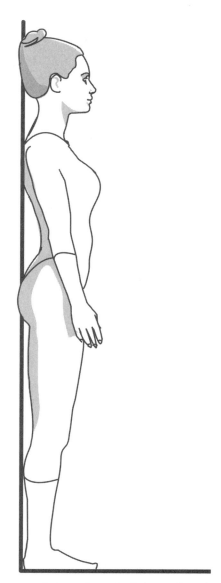

Spine elongated, but relaxed

Neutral Head Position

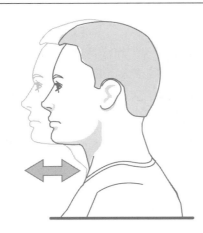

1. Glide your head forward as far as it will go.
2. Keeping your head level, glide back, pulling your chin toward your chest without dropping down.
3. Release to a position in between so that your ears are aligned with your shoulders.

You're in a neutral posture when your ears are aligned with your shoulders, shoulders with hips, hips with knees, and knees with ankles.

DEEP BREATHING

Inhale

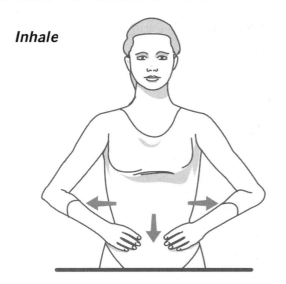

Exhale

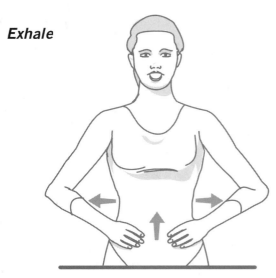

1. Standing in front of a mirror, inhale fully so your waist expands all the way around your body, including into your back. There should be no movement in your upper chest near your armpits.

2. In order to expel air to sing, your abdominal muscles contract slightly, causing your diaphragm to arch up against your lungs, pushing the air out of your lungs.

3. Try to keep your body open and don't collapse. If you push too hard with your abdominals, you will force all of your air out too fast. This action should be gentle and firm, with an emphasis on keeping your body open as you exhale.

KEEP YOUR RIBS OPEN

As you get to the end of your air supply, you'll feel the urge to squeeze your ribs and collapse your chest to expel the last of your air. However, good breathing technique dictates that you try to maintain an open chest and ribcage to the end of your breath. This will help you avoid becoming tense.

Try to keep your ribs open, even if you feel you're at the very end of your breath. Some describe this feeling as always maintaining a cushion of air under the ribs as you exhale. If you totally empty your lungs of every last bit of air, you are more likely to add pressure to your throat muscles. This creates strain in those muscles and will limit the freedom of your voice.

A QUIET BREATHING EXERCISE

1. Stand in front of a full-length mirror.
2. Take a deep breath with no chest lift (don't overfill), and hiss on a sustained "S" sound for as long as you can.
3. You will feel firmness in your abdominal muscles as you expel your air.
4. At the very end of your air supply, be sure to keep your ribs open and your chest in a comfortably high position.

Repeat two or three times, watching carefully to maintain good form. When you memorize good form by watching yourself, you are teaching your muscles to "remember" this action for singing.

Chapter 3. The Four P's: Essential Building Blocks for Vocal Training

THE FOUR ESSENTIAL BUILDING BLOCKS for vocal training are practice, patience, perseverance, and play. The "Four P's" are a good way to remember how to achieve balance in your studies.

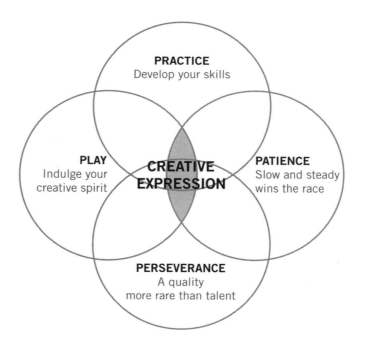

PRACTICE
Develop your skills

PLAY
Indulge your
creative spirit

CREATIVE
EXPRESSION

PATIENCE
Slow and steady
wins the race

PERSEVERANCE
A quality
more rare than talent

PRACTICE

Practicing is the way singers develop skills. Singers with well-developed instruments can be more expressive. Regular practice can help fine-tune the craft of singing and maintain a high level of skill, so the technique supports the expressive process. Without a sufficient skill base, or foundation, there can be no deep emotional or physical base on which to build. This is like the proverbial building constructed on sand. A weak foundation creates an unstable building that won't stand the test of time. Effective practice can build a strong foundation of technique that can help support a powerful voice. A full, strong, self-assured voice that has stamina can have the ability to express any emotion. In short, a strong foundation makes it possible to use your voice to its fullest capacity of creative expression.

COMPONENTS OF COMPLETE PRACTICE

Your practice routine ideally should consist of four parts:

1. Warm-up: Physical and Vocal
2. Technical Work
3. Song Performance
4. Cool Down

Physical Warm-ups

Stretching allows your body to move more efficiently and perform at its peak. It can release residual tension in your shoulders, neck, jaw, and back that you might not be aware of. Setting up good posture will increase your breath capacity. It's also an extremely soothing way to connect your mind and body, and it just feels good!

Mistakes to avoid:

- Don't bounce. Using bouncing to increase your stretch can activate your body's protective reflex, causing muscles to contract instead of stretch.
- Don't stretch to the point of pain. Slight discomfort when stretching is normal, but you should not be in pain. Pain is your body's signal that something is wrong.
- Don't forget to breathe. Oxygen exchange is necessary for muscles to respond to stretching in a beneficial way. Holding your breath will interfere with the relaxing effects of full oxygen intake and release. Use deep breathing as a way to heighten the stretching process.

Stretches

Start with these physical stretches.

Stretch 1. Spine Stretch

1. Reach both arms above your head, with hands crossed and palms touching.

2. Inhale, slowly pushing your hands upward, then backward, keeping your back straight.

3. Exhale and relax from the stretch before you repeat.

Stretch 2. Shoulder Stretch

1. Raise one arm above your head, and bend your elbow so that your fingers point down your spine.

2. Use your other hand to grasp your elbow above your head.

3. Exhale slowly, pulling gently down on your elbow, aiming your fingers down your spine.

4. Repeat on the other side.

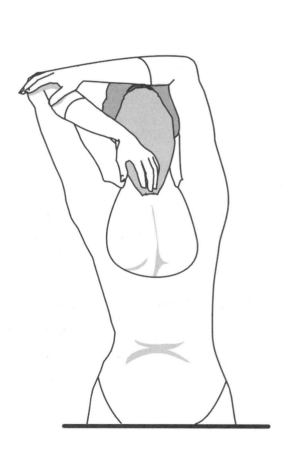
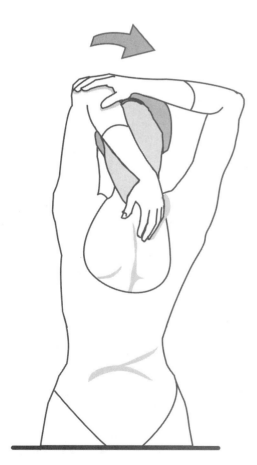

Stretch 3. Shoulder Rolls

1. Stand upright with your hands by your sides.

2. Lift your shoulders so that they are up by your ears.

3. Rotate them forward.

4. Continue rotation downward.

5. Move up and back in a smooth, continuous motion, and then return to rest position.

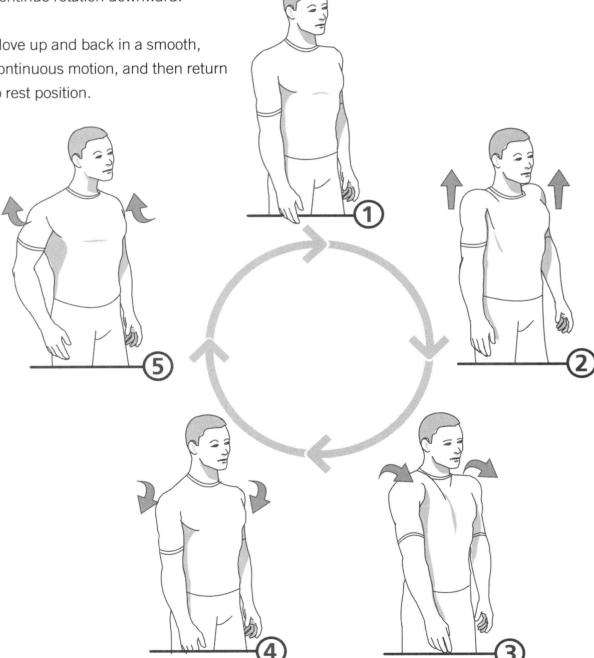

Vocal Warm-ups

Once you've stretched out your body, get ready to warm up your voice. To do this, put on the CD, and sing along with tracks 2–7, the Warm-ups for All Voices.

The most important thing you can do before you sing is warm up your voice. Vocal warm-ups are the physical equivalent of stretching your legs before you run. A gentle vocal warm-up will help your voice feel more flexible and responsive. It will also help you get the basics of breathing in place, reminding your muscles to produce the proper action. Warming up will also gently increase your range to its fullest capacity, so when you go for the high notes, your voice will feel freer. The exercises on the CD start in the middle voice. They help warm up the low range, then the high.

Here are some sounds commonly used for warming up. Try some of these before you go to more structured scale work to help warm up your voice. All of these sounds are demonstrated on the CD in the warm-up routines (tracks 2–7).

Exercise	Technique	Benefits
Lip/tongue trills	A bubbling sound made with lips or tongue. Can be used with scales or sliding.	Lip and tongue trills require a loose jaw and steady airflow; both beneficial to free tone production.
Sliding or siren sounds	Moving your voice up or down, gliding seamlessly through a series of pitches without stopping on scale notes. Sounds like a siren. Use any vowel, or hum.	Helps free up laryngeal muscles. Requires smooth muscular movement, gently stretching muscles involved in singing.
Humming	Creating tone with lips closed over teeth that are slightly apart. A buzzing feeling results in the lips, nose, face, and cheeks. Can be used with sliding (above).	The buzzing feeling produced when humming increases your awareness of resonance. Resonance amplifies and colors tone, making it brighter, with better projection.
Sighing	Start with a feeling that you're about to yawn. Make a vocal sound ("ah" or "uh") on a midrange pitch, allowing your voice to glide downward with a release of air.	The "pre-yawn" feeling helps lift your soft palate slightly, making a more open sound. The following downward glide releases your voice freely and allows a gentle muscle stretch.

Technique

Now that you're on your way to loosening up your voice, it's time to work on some voice-building exercises. Choose a Complete Vocal Workout on the CD, and sing along. Try to develop a variety of singing skills, such as better breath management, flexibility, and range extension. Stop if you feel tired or if you're straining in any way.

Here are some commonly used vocal technique exercises, elements of which are included in the workouts in part II. Use these ideas to better understand the benefits of each exercise pattern and to vary your routine.

Long Tones

Technique: Sustain a clear (not breathy) midrange tone for sixteen beats at a slow tempo. Tone should be at a medium-loud volume. Can also be used with dynamic variation: soft-loud-soft. Pitch should not waver.

Benefits: Long tones require efficient use of breath. A low intake of air and controlled exhalation, keeping the ribs from collapsing, will help coordinate and strengthen muscles used for breathing.

Runs/Scales

Technique: Sing stepwise note-patterns at a medium-fast to fast pace.

Benefits: Develops agility by training the vocal muscles to respond quickly and in a coordinated manner.

Staccato Exercises

Technique: Sing short, detached notes on a single breath, letting your air out a bit at a time. Staccato notes can be repeated single notes or in arpeggio or scale patterns.

Benefits: Develops agility and breath control requiring quick adjustments of the vocal cords. Staccato notes are to be sung lightly and articulated on the breath.

Arpeggios

Technique: Sing skipping-note patterns that outline chords. Arpeggios are typically built on major chords, minor chords, and pentatonic patterns.

Benefits: Develops facility in moving through entire range, easing register transitions, extending range and requiring flexibility and breath control.

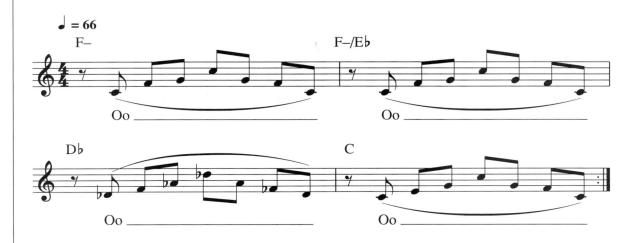

Articulation Exercises

Technique: Use the five primary vowels (a, e, i, o, u) combined with various consonants on musical patterns, creating nonsense syllables, such as "ma," "loo," "noh," "see," "yah," "nay," etc.

Benefits: Helps develop articulation skills. Also, various vowels and consonant combinations practiced throughout one's range develop facility and ease in tone production.

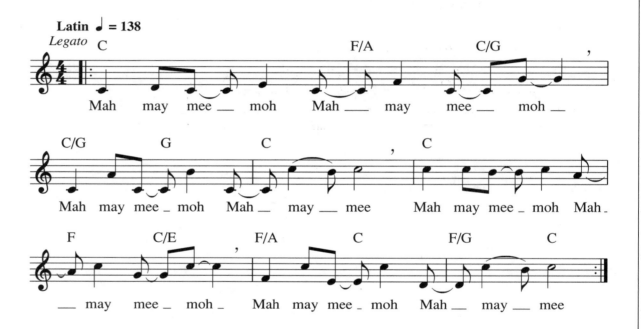

Dynamic Contrast

Technique: Sing a midrange long tone over eight slow counts, gradually becoming louder, then softer. Carefully pace the increasing and decreasing volume so it occurs smoothly, and so the pitch doesn't waver.

Benefits: Develops vocal control and increases awareness of dynamic contrast. Singing softly requires extra attention to maintaining consistent breath energy. Skillful singing at different dynamic levels will help you sing in tune more consistently.

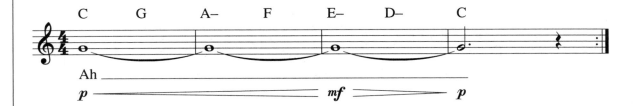

Range Extension Exercises

Technique: Sing fast-moving musical patterns (scales and arpeggios), briefly touching on highest and lowest notes. Do not dwell at the extremes of your range.

Benefits: Helps develop vocal strength. Gradual stretching of range and developing your upper register creates the ability to use more vocal colors and balances your instrument. Greater freedom throughout your range allows you to sing more varied repertoire.

continue moving
by half steps

Song Performance

After you have worked with the CD, take some time to work out on a couple of songs. Choose any style that you like, and check the range to see if it's within your limits. To do this, look for the highest and lowest notes of the song. The majority of the song should be in the middle of your range. If your song has a couple of notes that seem a little high or low, you can work on them to see if they become easier in time. If too much of the song is outside your range, you're better off choosing a different song. Be sure to watch yourself in the mirror to check for expression and body alignment.

Experienced singers may already know how much body movement is appropriate for their performance. But while you're developing or refreshing your technique, just stand and sing. Later on, when your technique is solidly established, you can focus on the song lyrics for the expression of emotions and ideas. This will free you up to use your hands and body more. Once you are able to focus on lyrics without diminishing your vocal skills, you'll be able to present your music with personal style and good vocal technique. If you accompany yourself on guitar or keyboard, practice your singing unaccompanied first, and progress to self-accompanied singing as you gain vocal skills.

Practice first without a microphone to establish good projection and resonance awareness. Be sure you're not relying on the microphone to create warm tone and projection. You have to develop these qualities as a part of your own vocal skills, to use with or without amplification.

Cool Down

Spend about five minutes doing some less intense vocal exercises to cool down your voice. Tracks 2 and 3 from the Warm-up for All Voices can be repeated to cool down. This will help your speaking voice sound more stable, and ease the transition from very active singing to a more normal state for everyday vocal use by allowing the tissue temperature to lower. This is similar to what we should do after vigorous physical exercise. After any kind of aerobic exercise, it is advisable to transition gradually so that the muscles can adjust to the change in heart rate. After a lot of singing, the increased blood flow to the vocal cords needs time to decrease gradually. During cool down, the laryngeal muscles also relax and return to a more neutral state. Cooling down also helps dissipate some of the normal fluid buildup that occurs when you sing. Cool-down exercises should involve light vocalizing in the middle to lower range. Descending lip trills are helpful for cooling down, as are sighs, descending slides on "oo," yawning that ends with an audible sigh, and light humming.

PATIENCE

Learning vocal technique requires patience, especially if there are bad habits to undo. The payoff for patience is having a well-trained instrument capable of greater expression. Most of the time, progress is gradual. Sometimes, we have "light bulb" moments in singing, but most of the time, progress comes after a long period of work that finally peaks, and then plateaus for a while. Sometimes, progress is made with two steps forward, then one step back, as we remind our muscles to memorize new actions and as we get used to different sounds and feelings. This is typical in the learning process for singing, and it requires a lot of patience.

Your voice will grow, change, and develop all through your life. Your voice will change as you age, and your sound will vary depending on how you feel and the state of your emotions. The changing nature of the human voice requires you to think beyond your immediate goals, such as song learning and breath management. So, be patient. Your best sound will continue to emerge and change as you develop.

PERSEVERANCE

Perseverance and patience go hand in hand. Musicians, actors, singers, and other artists know that while pursuing goals, we must keep in mind a bigger picture of what we want to achieve. With the many natural ups and downs in most singers' progress, it is important to stay determined. Whether you are dealing with the sense of disappointment after an unsatisfying performance, or just learning to enjoy using your voice to express yourself, keep trying to do your best.

PLAY

In the process of learning, it is easy to become worried about all the things that you haven't yet achieved. Remember that singing should be fun.

Devote a portion of every practice session to singing just for fun. Try sing-along recordings or karaoke. Turn off your critical thinking for a while, and just enjoy expressing yourself through music.

When you're developing your voice, you should practice what you *can* do, not just what you *can't* do.

Chapter 4. Vibrato, Vocal Registers, and Belting

OCAL WORKOUTS WILL BRING YOUR ATTENTION to different parts of your voice that you may not have noticed before. Vibrato, vocal registers, and belting are three important issues singers notice more when they are working out. Attention to these might help answer any questions that occur as you develop your voice.

VIBRATO

Vibrato is the steady oscillation (a wave-like sound) above and below a pitch center. It is created in the larynx by the alternating currents of nerve impulses and usually occurs naturally in voices that have balanced support and freedom of the muscles in the throat, neck, and jaw. If you don't have vibrato and you want to develop it, most voice teachers will start by working on breath support and releasing excessive tension.

It is helpful to have an awareness of your own vibrato and how to develop and control it when necessary. Although some singers don't use vibrato at all, many want at least a little to round out their sound. A healthy vibrato can be produced when a voice has a balance of adequate breath energy (or support) and relaxation. Vibrato speed and width can vary depending on the pitch or volume of the sound being produced.

There is a wide range of acceptable vibrato sounds. Most singers who want vibrato can develop it on their own, as their voices become balanced. The sound of a vibrato is a part of what singers hear and tend to imitate in voices on recordings, so it comes without effort to many young singers. On the other hand, singers with a persistently straight tone who want to develop vibrato need to be sure they release excess tension.

Classically trained singers frequently need to learn to control vibrato and sing with more straight tone when performing contemporary commercial music. This can be difficult, but it is a necessary skill in order to sing with authentic style in many genres of non-classical music.

Practice this by singing the long-tone exercise here. Imagine that you send a thin stream of air to the center of the tone to control vibrato.

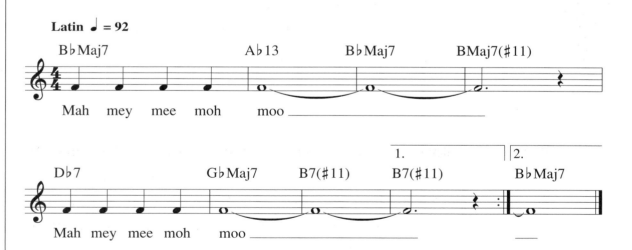

REGISTERS

Most singers are keenly aware of shifting in their voices as they sing up or down. These areas in your voice are called "registers." This shifting feeling often results in a change in sound quality.

When you sing, your vocal cords and larynx go through many adjustments in order to be able to produce different types of sound. Vocal cords vibrate at different lengths and thicknesses in different registers. For example, in chest register, there is light tension along both the length and width of your vocal cords. The higher you sing, the more the tension increases as the thickness decreases, so your vocal cords thin out as you ascend in pitch. At the same time, your arytenoid cartilages adjust to shorten your vocal cords for the change to head voice register. The shifting you feel is this complex series of muscles making the changes necessary for you to sing with different tone qualities. These adjustments can happen smoothly if your laryngeal muscles are coordinated, and the other aspects of your vocal technique are balanced. Because we can't see our vocal cords, using imagery and singing by "feel" are important methods in learning.

Try this sliding exercise. The slide should feel smooth and flow to the next pitch without any obvious bumps or changes in register.

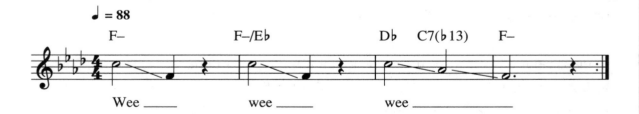

There are many different names for these registers, and quite a few opinions about how many registers there are and at what pitches the shifting occurs. Many rock, pop, r&b, and gospel singers—both men and women—audibly shift registers in their songs for stylistic effect. Shifting registers smoothly can help you access higher pitches without strain and can help you to achieve a certain color or style of expression. Your voice doesn't need to sound exactly the same from top to bottom, but it should be smooth enough that it's difficult to tell where the shifting occurs, unless you're yodeling. *Yodeling* is the technique of accentuating a change between registers very quickly, flipping to head or chest register with a stark change of vocal quality.

For women, *chest* voice is the lowest register, *head* voice is the upper register, and *middle* voice is a mix of the two in between. According to the book *Singing: the Mechanism and the Technique* by William Vennard, because the heavy mechanism (chest register) is two-thirds of the lower range, and the light mechanism (head register) is two-thirds of the higher range, either mechanism can be involved for the middle third of the voice.[1] With training, the middle register can be extended and strengthened, establishing a blend between low and high registers. This mix provides the flexibility needed for singing all styles of music.

Some women also have an additional register above head voice that's very light and fluty sounding, often called the *flute register*. This is the sound that Mariah Carey makes on her very highest tones, particularly in her early recordings.

In classical music, women mostly sing in a head-register-dominant sound. This creates a pure, balanced tone that gives the singer endurance, high range, and strong projection without electronic amplification. Vibrato is a predominant characteristic of Western European classical style singing, as well.

In non-classical singing, women are likely to use a *middle-, mixed-,* or *chest*-register-dominant sound. A microphone can diminish the need for vigorous projection of sound for ballad singing, and will amplify voices to project over other electronically amplified

---

1. Vennard, William. *Singing: the Mechanism and the Technique.* New York: Carl Fischer, 1967; p. 238.

instruments. The development of your upper register is important, even if it is not your primary performing register.

Men usually have a sense of where their chest register shifts into *falsetto,* a very high and light sounding register, which is a man's highest register. Men have head and middle registers as well, but they are often less obvious feeling than chest register and falsetto. If you're not sure what falsetto sounds like, listen to singers Aaron Neville, Smokey Robinson, Prince, and Al Jarreau. They, and many other singers, use their falsetto register frequently. Finding a light head-register sound without going into falsetto can be a challenge for men, but it is a very valuable and rewarding skill that can be used in a wide variety of contemporary music styles. This can best be achieved with the help of a vocal technique teacher who can help you discover and develop your full range.

If women can sense head register and chest registers in their voices, and men can sense chest register and falsetto, it's a good place to start. From there, work to develop your middle register. A strong middle register will give you the best of both worlds: some of the warmth of your lower register, and the ease of your upper register. Such skills are best learned in private voice lessons where a teacher can give you immediate feedback about your singing and help to correct any mistakes before they become detrimental.

Some voice qualities that might be considered unacceptable in classical singing can be appreciated for their uniqueness in popular music. Voice sounds such as twang (a bright, nasal tone that can facilitate belting), growls (a throaty rumble sometimes used at the beginnings of phrases), and glottal fry (a rapid series of low-pitched pulses, creating a creaky quality) are used to create sounds that are more speech-like. Although these sounds would be considered inappropriate to use in classical singing, in non-classical singing, these sounds are used to color tone and create style. Use these non-traditional sounds with discretion, though, as they can tire out your vocal cords.

BELTING

Contemporary commercial music singers often use *belting* as a style of singing. Belting generally refers to the act of singing loudly with a lot of energy. It can also refer to the specific technique of carrying up or mixing the chest register's quality, delaying the full release into head voice. This quality is similar to *speech-level singing,* which means carrying a speech quality high into the singing range. Belting usually requires more sound projection. Both speech-level singing and belting require a high breath pressure and a clear, strong sound. This sound can be strident when performed improperly at the highest pitch levels.

Belting can be accomplished in a healthy manner with careful attention to maintaining a resonant tone, breathing, and maintaining muscular relaxation in the neck and jaw. However, it can lead to vocal problems such as hoarseness and even vocal nodules, if it's done improperly, or in singers who aren't careful about maintaining their overall physical health. Excessive tiredness, a lack of vital physical health, and singing too much—too loudly, too high, too long—can lead to vocal problems as well.

Remember: even if you are primarily a belter, you should be able to sing in your head voice too. In fact, strengthening head and middle voice registers generally improves the quality of the lower registers by introducing brighter overtones and flexibility on high notes. Think of your head register as the mother of your entire voice.[2] If it is strong, it will nurture your entire range. Even if your head voice is weak at first, it will become stronger with use.

Contemporary music singers need the same type of comprehensive training that classical singers receive. Vocal problems commonly associated with singing non-classical music are often caused by a lack of the training that is part of every classical singer's basic education. If non-classical singers do not obtain proper training, they are risking their voices, and will be ill-prepared for the demands of performing this music.

Sometimes, non-classical singers are fearful that their individuality will be compromised if they study vocal technique. Developing good vocal skills can benefit all types

2. Mary Barton-Saunders, Chair of the Musical Theater Department at Pennsylvania State University.

of singers without making their voices sound "classical." In fact, non-classical singers can benefit from the same instruction and corrective actions used with classical singers, including paying better attention to vocal health and hygiene, watching out for excessive tension, and maintaining a resonant tone.

The demands of singing require all performers to learn everything they can about their voices in order to make informed decisions and choices that will not be detrimental to their vocal health.

IN THE PROCESS OF WORKING OUT, you may notice some changes in your voice, so vocal maintenance is an important aspect of working out.

Not everyone reacts to medications, caffeine, or even vocal overuse the same way. While a cup of coffee might trigger the jitters, dry throat, or excess mucus production in some people, it might have little effect on others. You have to know yourself, your limits, and your triggers for vocal problems. *Remember: it's easier to prevent problems than to correct them once you've done damage.*

MAINTAINING VOCAL HEALTH

For professional vocalists, taking care of your voice is a primary responsibility. You will want to be able to sing not just when you're healthy and happy, but through adversity as well. When you have a cold, low physical energy, or stressful performing situations, you need to know how to use your acquired vocal technique to get through it all. It's even better if you can prevent problems by following some basic heathcare principles that will help you stay well. If you know how to take care of yourself, you'll be able to perform better under challenging circumstances.

Water

One of the easiest ways to improve your health is to be sure you are drinking eight 8-ounce glasses of water each day. Your body needs water to function well. Water flushes toxins out of your system and keeps the mucus thin in your throat. This can make for less throat clearing and coughing that will tire out your vocal cords. Water also helps keep your vocal cords supple. It's like having enough oil in your car engine. With lubrication, the parts of the engine glide instead of grind. In your singing, this means your voice will work more efficiently.

Your entire body needs to be hydrated for your vocal cords to function smoothly. Drink water well in advance of your vocal practice and performance. Caffeine and alcohol dry out your body and voice, countering the effects of water drinking. It's smart to limit these drying substances.

Many singers find that inhaling steam can be soothing, especially if you have a cold, or if you live in a dry environment. You can carefully heat plain water in a pan, and when it is hot, put a towel over your head to make a sort of a tent, and inhale the steam. (Be very careful that you don't stand too close to the heating element!) Instead, you can use a gadget called a "personal steam inhaler." It has a small reservoir for water and a mask that fits over your nose and mouth. When the water is heated, place your nose and mouth on or near the mask, and inhale the steam for ten to fifteen minutes several times a day. I recommend that you don't add anything to the water, such as menthol medications, because those can dry you out further. Just inhaling the steam can soothe your nasal passages and throat.

Don't Smoke

Smoking is bad for your voice. When you inhale the hot chemicals in cigarette or marijuana smoke over your vocal cords (which are located at the gateway to your lungs), you dry out and irritate them. The chemicals from smoke deposit in your lungs, making it harder to breathe deeply. Coughing further irritates your cords. Even inhaling second-hand smoke affects your health. So, don't smoke. Quit if you have already started. It will be well worth the trouble, in terms of increased lungpower and overall health. And avoid inhaling secondhand smoke.

Stress

Since our voices are closely linked with our emotions, stress can have a devastating effect on a singer's ability to perform. Instead of just trying to push through stressful times, try to find effective ways to alleviate your stress.

Dealing effectively with stress means that we consider the whole person, not just the voice. Physical activities including walking, swimming, yoga, tai chi, as well as quiet time, listening to relaxation tapes, and receiving professional counseling are all effective in relieving stress and anxiety.

Overall Health

Your voice reflects the state of your overall health. Your mind, body, and spirit together have a balanced relationship. When you are sick physically, or troubled emotionally, your voice will probably reflect these problems. Balance in all areas of your life can provide a fuller, more satisfying singing experience. Moderate exercise, healthy eating, relaxation techniques such as meditation, and regular sleeping habits are a good way to start.

DETECTING VOCAL PROBLEMS

When you're having problems with your voice, it can be frustrating and upsetting. Since we can't see our vocal cords just by looking in the mirror, we have to pay attention to symptoms that may indicate a problem. These symptoms may be early signs of injury or other problems and must not be ignored.

SIGNS OF POSSIBLE VOCAL PROBLEMS

- loss of high range or the loss of the ability to sing softly on high notes
- a strained, hoarse, or husky sound that persists for more than a few days
- hoarseness without any other symptoms (such as a cold)
- singing or speaking requires noticeable effort
- increased need for breath support
- repeated vocal fatigue or deterioration of your voice after singing
- a constant feeling of excessive mucus or a post-nasal drip
- a feeling of pain or irritation after singing
- any unusual long-term symptoms that affect your voice or overall health
- your intuition tells you that something is not right with your voice

IF YOU SUSPECT YOU HAVE A PROBLEM...

Consult a qualified laryngologist who specializes in treating professional singers. He or she will be able to advise you of your options for managing your vocal health. A laryngologist can tell you if you need medical treatment, or if you can ease your symptoms with home care. Most conservatories or music schools can recommend a laryngologist who specializes in working with singers.

Singing When You're Sick

If you have to perform and you're not feeling up to par, you will have to make a judgment call. Sometimes, a slightly scratchy throat and nasal congestion won't inhibit singing. If this is the case, a light warm-up will tell you if you should carry on. If you sing for fifteen to twenty minutes and your voice clears up, your high range is accessible, and you have enough energy to support adequately, you might be able to perform. Be sure to drink lots of water to keep the mucus in your throat thin and to help avoid excessive throat clearing and coughing. Inhalation of steam by placing your face over a source of warm steam (as described earlier) can help by directly moistening the surface of your vocal cords. However, if you're an inexperienced singer, leave this kind of judgment call to your teacher or a doctor.

On the other hand, a husky, pressed-sounding voice, and loss of high range that doesn't improve with a light warm-up can signify a more serious condition. It's best to consult a doctor right away if you have any questions about your vocal health.

Avoid taking pain medicines when you're performing. You can easily over-sing and end up hurting your voice because the pain medications interfere with your perception of your vocal condition. You won't be able to feel if you're over-singing, and then you can lose your voice completely. Also, aspirin and Ibuprofen can make the capillaries in your vocal cords fragile and more susceptible to breaking. Hard singing paired with medicines that stop pain and promote fragile capillaries is a recipe for serious vocal problems.

Chapter 6. Auditioning

MOST SINGERS ARE AWARE of the close connection between our emotions and our ability to sing well under challenging circumstances. If you're working out your voice to prepare for an audition, here are some tips to help you through this demanding situation.

Whether you're new to performing or have a lot of experience, you'll probably have to audition for a gig or otherwise be evaluated by others in the industry. If you are prepared for criticism and maintain the right attitude, you can learn and grow from the process. You might come away from a performance where you've received feedback that was right on target, and that evaluation can help you improve your singing. It is understandable that criticism meant in the spirit of helpfulness can surprise you and might hurt your feelings. But if you are prepared mentally, these experiences can have excellent learning potential.

TAKING CRITICISM IN STRIDE

If you have an audition or performance experience in which you feel you have done your best and you still don't receive positive feedback, consider other aspects of your performance that may need improvement. Your presentation, singing skill, movement, and lyric delivery all can affect your audition. Also, sometimes, auditioners are looking for a specific "look" or physical type, and if you don't fit that image, you can be ruled out. As harsh as this sort of elimination can be, it is a fact of many auditions, and persistence and hard work can be the key to getting the gig you want.

AUDITIONS GONE BAD

Sometimes, auditions just don't go well. Nervousness, lack of preparation, performing a song that doesn't flatter your voice, and many other issues can affect your performance. You might receive well-deserved negative feedback. Vow to be better prepared next time, and practice performing in front of others. Record yourself doing a mock audition on videotape. You might be surprised at habitual body or hand movements that are distracting. You might also hear mistakes in your singing that you weren't aware of. Some singers say that when they're performing, they feel as if they're using a lot of great facial expression, but when they see their recorded performance, they are surprised to see that their expression is blank. Videos will give you unbiased feedback. It isn't always fun to watch yourself, but it is one of the best ways you can improve your performing skills.

YOU NEVER KNOW WHO'S WATCHING

Present yourself at your best every time you perform because you never know who will see you and remember you. Even if auditioners aren't looking for someone with your skills at that time, there is always a chance that they will remember a good, charismatic performer and hire you in the future. Many singers get gigs because someone remembers them from another performance, audition, or gig and wants to hire them at a later date. So don't lose hope if you don't get the gig the first time. It may lead to something better farther down the road. You have to be true to yourself. Be the best performer you can be. Discover your unique qualities and show them off! Don't just try to imitate your favorite singer; discover your own true voice. Be persistent, always present yourself at your best, and learn from honest criticism. If you are having trouble handling criticism, or feel unfairly treated, talk to someone who can help you put things into perspective. Keeping negative thoughts bottled up inside or obsessing over negative comments is not productive or healthy. Consider the subjective nature of auditions, and let the experience create an opportunity for you to improve.

- Warm-ups for All Voices

- Workout 1. Basic Workout

- Workout 2. Advanced Workout

- Singing Harmony: Two- and Three-Part
  Exercises

COMPLETE VOCAL WORKOUTS

PART

FEATURES OF THE CD

These exercises provide a complete warm-up and basic and advanced voice-building exercises for singers. The CD contains vocal examples with a rhythm-section background. The vocal examples appear on only one stereo side of the CD so that you can sing along with them, or turn them off to practice with the rhythm section tracks alone. To listen and practice with the rhythm section alone, adjust the balance control on your stereo to eliminate the right channel. If you transfer the CD to an MP3 player to practice, you can simply remove the right ear bud to hear only the instruments. Even if you don't have easy balance adjustment capabilities on your computer, you can still benefit from singing with the voices on the recording. The singers demonstrate authentic style and phrasing models. I feel that it is important for you to hear real voices performing the examples. Singers who have worked with this CD have found the vocal guidelines helpful, and often keep the voices sounding even when they are familiar with the exercises.

At the beginning of each track, you'll hear a beginning note and a countoff, and then the exercise begins. You might find it helpful to follow along with the written music in the book until you become familiar with the exercise patterns, the order in which they occur in each workout, and the syllables and lyrics used for singing.

If you are working on particularly challenging exercises, especially those in the Advanced Workout, you can go back to the start of the track to review it a few times before moving on.

Sometimes, the exercises move up by half steps to new keys, and sometimes they modulate down, depending on what part of your voice is being exercised. You'll be able to follow along easily listening to the instrumentals. When warming up, it is best to warm up your middle range first, then low voice, followed by high range warm-up. This plan is followed in the Warm-up for All Voices.

The Basic Workout will help you take your singing to the next level. Musical concepts such as syncopation, minor scales, and pentatonic patterns are presented in rock, jazz, r&b, and gospel style exercises. These are designed to help you develop your range, flexibility, and sustaining power.

The Advanced Workout contains more complex rhythmic concepts, more challenging intervallic leaps, as well as longer phrases. Be sure to maintain energetic breath support, and don't push yourself beyond your limits, especially the first few times you sing through this workout. Change the syllables or words to a favorable vowel, such as "oo" or "ah," until you become familiar with the notes and rhythmic patterns.

In high- and low-voice workouts, you will alternately hear male and female voices demonstrate the exercises. Notice that a man's voice always sounds one octave lower than written on the treble clef. This is a concept that most singers adjust to automatically, without much thought. If you are a man, and a woman is demonstrating the exercise, you should sing the exercise in your own octave (one octave lower than the woman's voice). If you try to sing in her octave, you will probably be singing high in your range, or in falsetto, and you won't gain the benefits of low- to middle-voice exercises. If you are a woman, and a man is demonstrating the exercise, you should sing one octave higher than the man's voice.

The Two- and Three-Part Exercises on the last section of the CD are a fun bonus to your singing workouts. By adjusting your balance control, the different voices on these tracks can be individually eliminated for practice. Turn off the left channel to eliminate the high voice. Turn off the right channel to eliminate the low voice. In the three-part exercises, there are two tracks of each exercise. Again, turn off the left channel to eliminate the high voice. Turn off the right channel to eliminate the low voice. Go to the second track to hear the track without the middle voice part.

After you work with the CD a few times, you might find that the key ranges of some of the exercises suit your voice better in a higher or lower workout, depending on the style of the exercise. For example, if you are a tenor or soprano, you might discover that the exercises in the low voice workouts fit your voice better. You might even put together a combination of some of the high and some of the low exercises to create your own personal workout. The key is to try both high and low workouts to find what works best for you.

As you follow the CD's vocal workouts, remember these tips:

- Watch yourself in a mirror. Look for good posture, facial expression, and signs of tension.
- Expand around your waist when you breathe. There should be no movement in your upper chest. Even quick breaths need to expand around your waist, not at chest level.
- Stop immediately if you feel that you're becoming tired or straining in any way.
- Keep a bottle of water at hand to help stay hydrated.

THIS WARM-UP ROUTINE will help prepare your voice for singing. It is like stretching your legs before you run. Various vowel sounds are introduced, as well as the lip trill, which can be very effective in balancing your airflow and bringing your attention to the buzzing feeling associated with tone that is resonating efficiently—what singers call "forward placement."

EXERCISE 1. WARM-UP SLIDE

This exercise will help you to warm up your middle voice. Lip trills combined with sliding help induce laryngeal freedom, and help gently stretch your singing muscles.

A lip trill is a loose bubbling sound made with the lips. Imitate the sound of a motor-boat by blowing out air, letting your lips bubble, first with no vocal sound, then adding voice.

Lip trills require a loose jaw and steady air pressure. If you have trouble doing lip trills, perform this exercise by rolling or trilling your tongue instead.

Sing five times modulating up by half steps.

♩ = 92

Ab	Ab/G	F–	Eb Eb/G

1. Brrr (lip thrill)   brrr _____   brrr _____
2. Oo _____   oo _____   oo _____
3. Ee _____   ee _____   ee _____
4. Brrr _____   brrr _____   brrr _____
5. Ee _____   ee _____   ee _____

Ab	Ab/G	F– Db	Ab

Brrr _____   brrr _____   brrr _____
Oo _____   oo _____   oo _____
Ee _____   ee _____   ee _____
Brrr _____   brrr _____   brrr _____
Ee _____   ee _____   ee _____

EXERCISE 2. DESCENDING FIFTH SLIDE

This exercise will help you to warm up your middle and lower voice. Sliding helps free up your voice by gently stretching the muscles before you sing. To slide, make a siren sound starting in your middle range, and glide down without stopping on individual pitches.

Sing this exercise six times, modulating down by half steps each time. Alternate the syllables "wee" and "zoo" until the end.

TIPS

- The position of your throat just before you yawn helps you open up for freer singing. Imagine that open feeling as you slide.
- Be careful to tune the descending minor third in the last two bars. Keep your breath support active to avoid flatting the pitch.

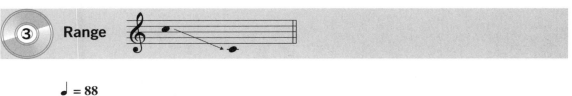

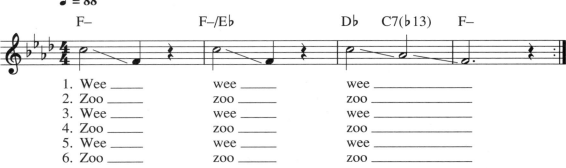

1. Wee _____	wee _____	wee _____
2. Zoo _____	zoo _____	zoo _____
3. Wee _____	wee _____	wee _____
4. Zoo _____	zoo _____	zoo _____
5. Wee _____	wee _____	wee _____
6. Zoo _____	zoo _____	zoo _____

EXERCISE 3. DESCENDING FIFTH RUN

This exercise will help develop flexibility needed to execute the quick moving scale, and the descending pattern helps establish relaxed production as you gradually increase range.

Singing on "Nee, nay, noh, noo" will help you find your best tone placement. Use the "N" to increase your awareness of resonating tone. You should feel a slight buzz in your cheeks or nose on this voiced consonant. If you prefer, substitute "M" on subsequent modulations.

Sing this exercise six times, modulating up by a half step each time.

TIPS

- Work for clean but smooth articulation of the descending-fifth pattern. Sing the pattern without separating the individual pitches. (Avoid "Nee-hee-hee-hee-hee.")
- Put the initial consonant on the pitch. Be careful that the descending pattern is supported with adequate breath energy so the pitch doesn't flat.

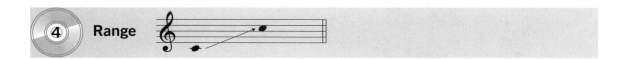

Nee _____ Nay _____ Noh _____ Noo _____

EXERCISE 4. POP/ROCK SLIDE

This exercise will help you to blend registers by sliding between notes. Continue the gentle stretching of your vocal cords by singing lightly and being careful to energize your breath support.

Work to blend your registers in this exercise by sliding between notes that are stepwise. This requires more vocal control than the previous slides, because you are connecting notes of the scale, but briefly stopping on each tone. On the ascending part of the scale, keep a steady flow of air to assist with the upward slide.

Experiment with other vowel sounds such as "nee," "yah," or lip trills, to equalize all vowels on this pattern. Try to sing all vowels freely.

Sing this exercise six times, ascending by half steps.

TIPS

- Try to sing each 4-bar phrase in one breath.
- Sing the last note of the 8-bar pattern short, allowing you to breathe as the key modulates.
- Minimize vibrato, keeping an even, steady tone.

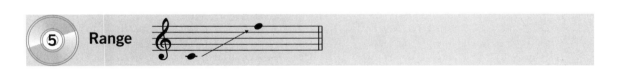

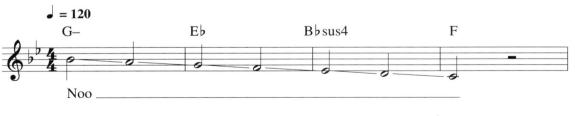

Noo _____

Noo _____

EXERCISE 5. DESCENDING ARPEGGIOS (SWING)

Warm up your middle and lower registers and further develop harmonic awareness by singing major descending arpeggios with changing harmonies. Sing each descending note with a slight jazz-style scoop, as demonstrated on the recording.

Change initial consonants to experiment with different onsets of the tone. Try "W," "M," and "Y" to increase your awareness of resonating tone. Are some consonants easier to start a tone on than others? Notice which consonants and vowels flow more easily, and try to make all of them equally free.

Sing this exercise five times, descending by half steps.

TIPS

- Sing this exercise in a swing style with a slight scoop at the start of each pitch, as demonstrated on the recording.
- Tune your voice to the changing harmonies by carefully listening and thinking while you sing.
- Keep breath support active, to avoid flat intonation.
- Take a relaxed breath, but don't overfill between phrases.

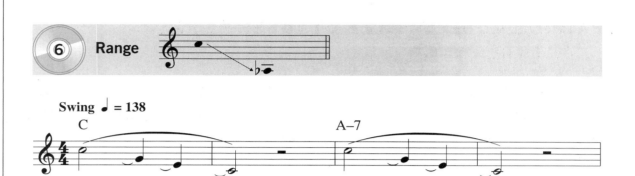

6 Range

Swing ♩ = 138

C   A–7

Nee _____   Nay _____

FMaj9   B♭Maj7(♯11)

Noh _____   Noo _____

C   A–7

Nee _____   Nay _____

FMaj9   FMaj7/G   C

Noh _____   Noo _____

EXERCISE 6. OCTAVE SLIDES

Finish warming up your middle-to-high range with slides, to blend registers. Using slides can help you access and warm up your high range because you won't be focused on sustaining the high note. You should just slide up, touch on the note, and slide back down.

Many singers find this exercise successful on "oo" vowels or lip trills. "Oo" helps lift your soft palate for easier access to your upper register. Also, singers tend to use a more consistent airflow when singing lip trills, instead of worrying about the pitches or tone quality. When you focus on breath rather than tone quality, you often can sing the high notes in your range more easily.

At the end of this exercise, the highest notes might be out of range for low voices. Continue with the modulations only as high as you feel comfortable. You can skip ahead to the next workout when you've reached your limit.

Sing this exercise five times, ascending by half steps.

TIPS

■ Keep your voice light, to ascend smoothly to the highest notes.

■ Imagine that your voice glides on a steady stream of breath.

■ Imagine the tone vibrating on your teeth, for forward placement.

■ Use no vibrato on slides, keeping the tone even and steady.

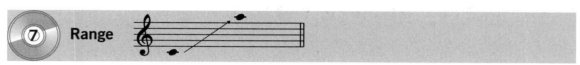

⑦ Range

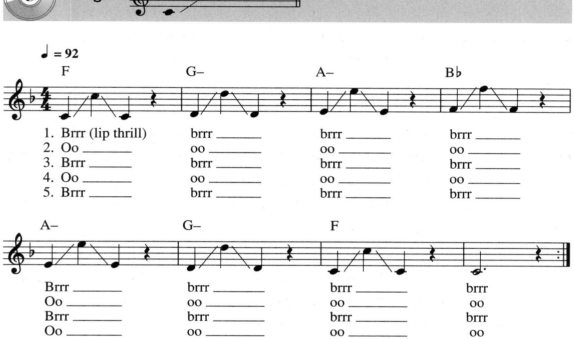

♩ = 92

F　　　　　　G–　　　　　　A–　　　　　　B♭

1. Brrr (lip thrill)　　brrr _____　　brrr _____　　brrr _____
2. Oo _____　　　　oo _____　　　oo _____　　　oo _____
3. Brrr _____　　　brrr _____　　brrr _____　　brrr _____
4. Oo _____　　　　oo _____　　　oo _____　　　oo _____
5. Brrr _____　　　brrr _____　　brrr _____　　brrr _____

A–　　　　　　G–　　　　　　F

Brrr _____　　　brrr _____　　brrr _____　　brrr
Oo _____　　　　oo _____　　　oo _____　　　oo
Brrr _____　　　brrr _____　　brrr _____　　brrr
Oo _____　　　　oo _____　　　oo _____　　　oo
Brrr _____　　　brrr _____　　brrr _____　　brrr

Workout 1. Basic Workout

THE BASIC WORKOUT is an essential voice-building workout. You will sing basic scales and patterns to build skills. Before you start the Basic Workout, warm up with tracks 2–7, stretch your body to release tension, and align your body with good posture.

For these exercises, low voices should use CD tracks 8–14; high voices should use CD tracks 22–28.

EXERCISE 7. ROCK STEPS

Work to develop flexibility for singing fast-moving notes and riffs on one continuous syllable.

Sing each 8-bar phrase in one breath, if possible. If you can't make it through on one breath, breathe after the dotted half note in bar 4.

Sing this exercise five times, modulating up diatonically.

TIPS

- For the final modulation, make up your own syllables or repeat previous syllables that feel and sound best in your voice.
- Use energetic breath support, and don't pulse air on each moving note. Your air should flow in a steady stream.

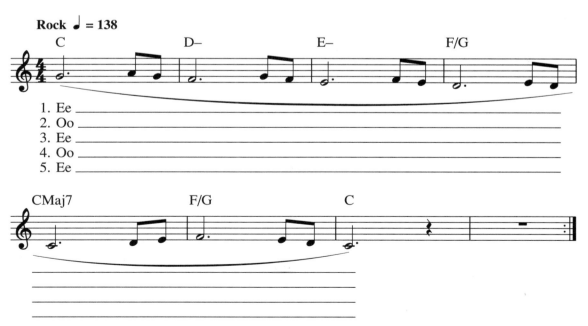

EXERCISE 8. ROCK SYNCOPATION

Develop coordination and a strong rhythmic concept by singing syncopated rhythms in a rock style. Syncopated rhythms accent an offbeat. Try to sing these rhythms without rushing.

Focus on your breath support, keeping gentle firmness in your abdominals. Don't push your abs too hard. Stay open in your ribs.

Sing this exercise five times, moving up by half steps.

TIPS

- Take a relaxed, quiet breath in the beginning of the exercise, and at the beginning of bar 4. Don't gasp or tighten up your throat for the quick breaths.
- Try different syllable combinations, such as doo-yah and way-oh. You can also make up your own scat syllable phrases. Be creative! (Avoid "scooby dooby doo," as it's a jazz cliché.)

EXERCISE 9. MINOR OCTAVE SCALE

Develop flexibility and extend your range singing on a minor scale pattern. Sing legato, using continuous, gentle air pressure. Be sure not to pulse on each individual note.

For ease in initiating tone, try using a voiced consonant at the beginning of each phrase. This will help you keep the tone vibrant and ringing. Try "N," "W," "M," "Y," or "L."

Sing this exercise six times, modulating up by half steps.

TIPS

- Breathe with a relaxed throat, being careful not to gasp.
- Keep your chest comfortably high and your ribs open as you sing. Don't collapse as you use your air supply.

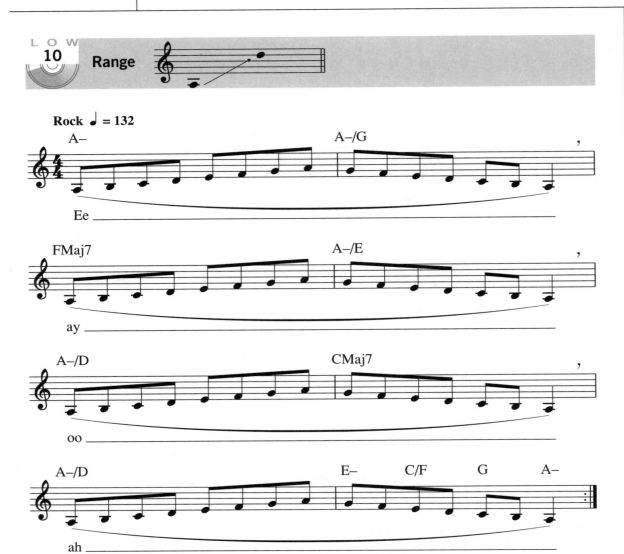

24
HIGH

Range

Rock ♩ = 132

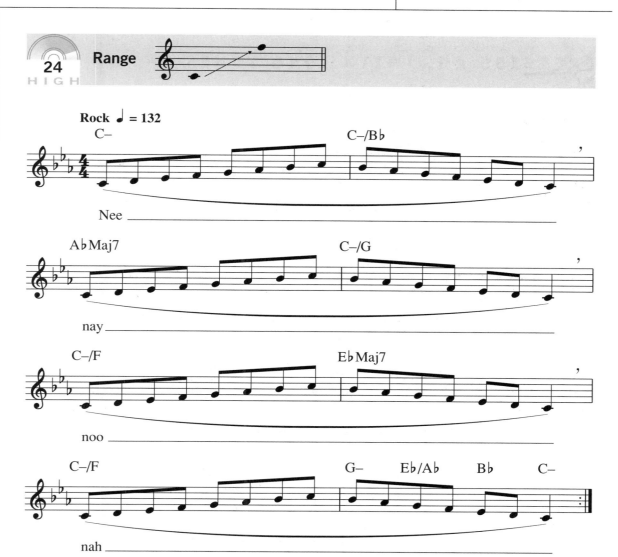

C–

C–/B♭

Nee

A♭Maj7

C–/G

nay

C–/F

E♭Maj7

noo

C–/F

G– E♭/A♭ B♭ C–

nah

EXERCISE 10. LATIN LONG TONES

Work to extend your breath control to sing the long phrases in this exercise. Deep breaths expanding around your waist paired with consistent opening of your ribs will give you better control over long phrases.

Use the initial consonant to place the tone forward in your mouth. Try to feel a buzz on your lips and nose on the "M." This will help establish forward placement to make a resonant, clear tone that doesn't waste your breath.

Sing this exercise five times, modulating up diatonically.

TIPS

■ Check your body alignment, and be sure your chest doesn't collapse, especially as the exercise reaches the higher pitch levels.

■ Challenge yourself by adding a controlled crescendo and decrescendo within each 4-bar phrase.

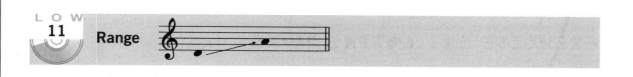

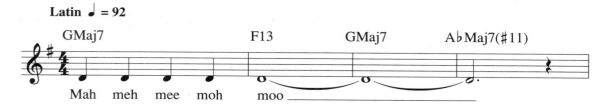

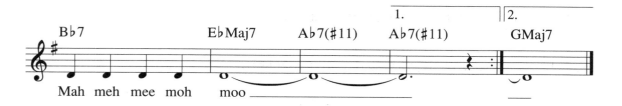

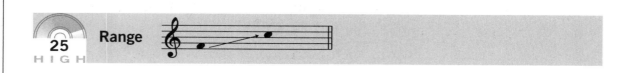

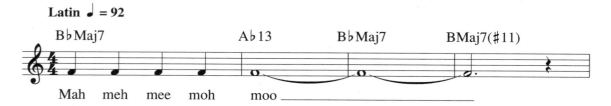

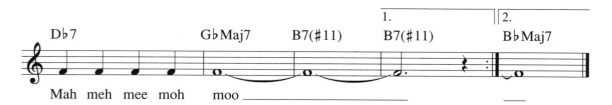

EXERCISE 11. GOSPEL SWING

This exercise will help you develop a good rhythmic concept for singing swing eighth notes and minor arpeggios with basic scat syllables. Make sure that the second note in the eighth-note pair occurs on the last third of the beat. The arpeggios outline a minor chord and are easily tuned with careful listening.

Sing this exercise three times, modulating up by whole steps.

TIPS

- Don't rush the swing eighth notes. Keep them loose and relaxed.
- Use the scat syllables in the example, making sure that you don't over-pronounce. The syllables should sound relaxed.

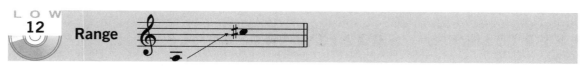

12 Range

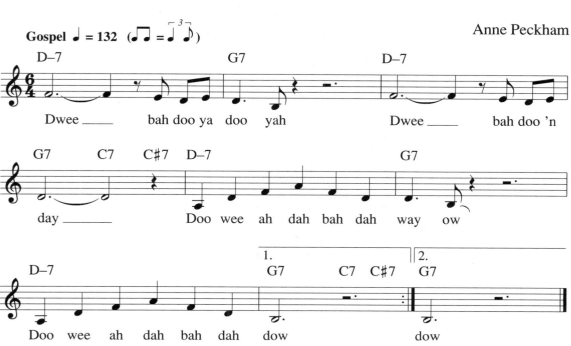

Gospel ♩ = 132

Anne Peckham

Dwee _____ bah doo ya doo yah   Dwee _____ bah doo 'n

day _____   Doo wee ah dah bah dah way ow

Doo wee ah dah bah dah dow   dow

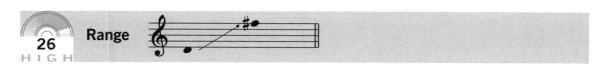

26 Range

Gospel ♩ = 132

Anne Peckham

Dwee _____ bah doo ya doo yah   Dwee _____ bah doo 'n

day _____   Doo wee ah dah bah dah way ow

Doo wee ah dah bah dah dow   dow

EXERCISE 12. JAZZ SWING SCALE

Continue to explore a swing eighth-note feel in this exercise with scat syllable articulation. You will also be working on range extension. Work to increase breath control in order to sing the first eight bars in one breath. Add breaths at bars 4 and 12, if you can't sing this in two long 8-bar phrases yet.

Sing this exercise six times, modulating up by half steps.

TIPS

- Keep the articulation of the scat syllables forward in your mouth, at the tip of your tongue. Articulate lightly in a relaxed manner.
- Lighten up your voice as you ascend, for ease on the highest notes.

13 Range

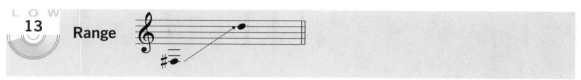

Jazz Swing ♩ = 144

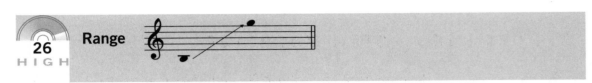

EXERCISE 13. LATIN VOCALISE

This exercise will help develop agility and flexibility with dynamic contrast. Sing this exercise with a light, dancing feel. Use any syllable or combination of syllables that you like. Or better yet, create your own lyrics.

Coordinate breaths as marked in music. Don't skip breath marks. You might end up straining, or become out of breath in the middle of a phrase.

Use varied dynamics that follow the shape of the melody (softer on lower notes, louder on higher notes), building to mezzo-forte in the bridge of the song.

The etude is performed twice on the CD: once with the vocal, then the second time featuring just the instrumentals, to give you a chance to try the piece without the lead vocal line.

TIPS

- Sing with straight eighth notes throughout.
- Eighth-note runs should flow evenly without pulsing air out on each note (not "nah-ha-ha-ha-ha").
- Try singing on "oo" as heard on track 14 or "ah" as on track 28.
- Watch out for the accidental in bar 24.

VOCAL WORKOUTS

FOR THE CONTEMPORARY SINGER

Workout 2. Advanced Workout

FOR SINGERS looking for more challenging range and flexibility exercises, the Advanced Workout will broaden your skills. If you are beginning your workout here, be sure to stretch your body, take a couple of deep diaphragmatic breaths to anchor your breathing, warm up your voice with the Warm-up for All Voices, then follow along with the next set of exercises. If you have already sung the Basic Workout and are continuing with the Advanced Workout, be sure you don't over do it, especially if you haven't been singing regularly. If any exercise feels out of your range, stop, and be sure you're not pushing.

This vocal workout requires more stamina, range, and stylistic acumen. Try to create a free, relaxed sound. Work to maintain energetic support so that your voice doesn't tire. Your energy should come from the center of your body, not from your throat. Maintain a loose jaw and neutral posture, and have fun!

EXERCISE 14. ROCK VOCALISE

This exercise will help you develop agility singing fast pentatonic patterns in a rock style. Pentatonic patterns are used in many styles of contemporary music, including r&b and rock. This exercise can also help you develop a basic vocabulary for improvising or embellishing melodies. Work for clean, accurate note articulation.

Sing this exercise three times, modulating each time up by a half step.

TIPS

- Keep a clear tone with no added rock-style grit to the sound.
- Sing the "H's" lightly so that you don't blow out too much air.
- Slight diaphragmatic accents will give the line kick, but don't punch too much with the breath. Bring your attention to maintaining steady breath support.

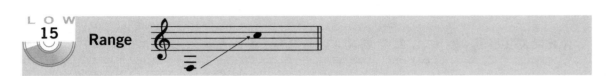

Anne Peckham

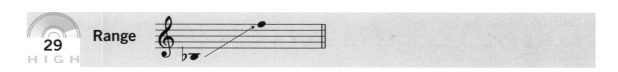

29
HIGH

Range

Anne Peckham

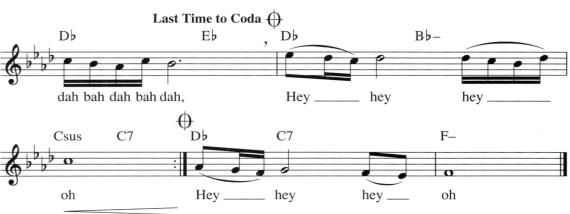

EXERCISE 15. LATIN OCTAVE SKIPS

This syncopated Latin style requires quick air intake. This exercise will help you develop coordination for quick breaths, as well as note accuracy for singing various intervals.

Sing this exercise three times, modulating up by half steps.

TIPS

- Work to keep your tone quality even and blended.
- Take quick breaths every two bars, keeping a relaxed throat. The breaths should be quiet, and the inhalation action should quickly expand at your waist.
- Put the consonant "M" exactly on the target pitch, with no scooping, to ensure accuracy.

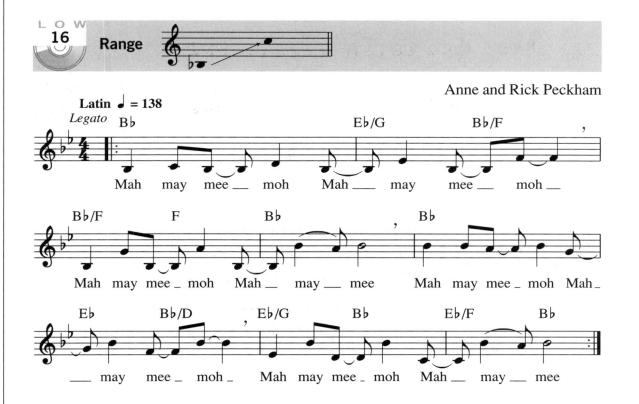

16 **Range**

Anne and Rick Peckham

Latin ♩ = 138

Legato

| Bb | Eb/G | Bb/F |

Mah may mee __ moh Mah __ may mee __ moh __

| Bb/F | F | Bb | Bb |

Mah may mee _ moh Mah __ may __ mee Mah may mee _ moh Mah_

| Eb | Bb/D | Eb/G | Bb | Eb/F | Bb |

__ may mee _ moh _ Mah may mee _ moh Mah __ may __ mee

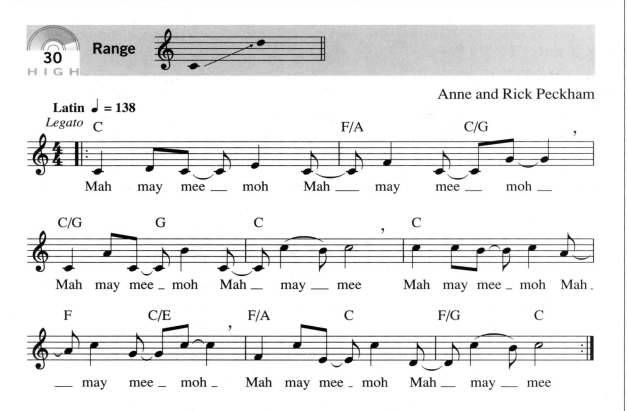

Anne and Rick Peckham

Latin ♩ = 138
Legato

Mah may mee __ moh Mah __ may mee __ moh __

Mah may mee _ moh Mah __ may __ mee Mah may mee _ moh Mah _

__ may mee _ moh _ Mah may mee _ moh Mah __ may __ mee

EXERCISE 16. JAZZ WALTZ ("MAYBE ON MONDAY")

This exercise will help develop note accuracy and range with ascending arpeggio patterns. The lyrics intentionally include many voiced consonants such as "M," "N," and "W." These consonants help you feel your voice resonate in your "mask" (cheeks, nose, forehead, teeth, and the front of your mouth).

Sing the entire piece two times through as written.

TIPS

- Lightly articulate the lyrics, keeping the consonants on the tip of your tongue.
- Be careful to sing the pickup notes to each phrase accurately. The tempo moves fast, and you have to think ahead the first few times you sing this to sing the pickups in tune.
- The etude is performed twice on the CD: once with the vocal, then the second time featuring just the instrumentals, to give you a chance to try the piece without the lead vocal line.

17 Range

Anne and Rick Peckham

Jazz Waltz ♩ = 183

Maybe on Monday, _____ maybe on Tues - day, _____ maybe on Wednes - day, _____ maybe not. _____ Will you on Monday, _____ will you on Tues - day, _____ will you on Wednes - day, _____ well, why not? _____ Never on Monday, _____ never on Tues - day, _____ never on Wednes - day, _____ thanks a lot. _____ Maybe on _____

Anne and Rick Peckham

EXERCISE 17. R&B POP/PENTATONIC ("WAIT FOR ME")

This exercise will help you develop agility and a strong rhythmic concept singing pentatonic patterns.

Notice that you enter on beat 2 in bars 1, 5, 9, etc. and that you enter on the "and" of the beat, or the upbeat, in bars 3, 4, 7, 8, etc. Count as you sustain the first long note in bars 1 and 2. (If you lose count, it will be difficult to make the next entrance correctly.)

Sing this exercise twice through, as written.

TIPS

- Watch for the syncopated entrances in the second half of each 4-bar phrase.
- Balance your voice so all notes blend and match in color.
- Sing at a slower tempo to study, and speed up to tempo as you learn the patterns.

18 **Range**

Anne Peckham

Anne Peckham

EXERCISE 18. R&B PENTATONIC PATTERN ("HEY YAH")

This exercise will help you develop agility singing pentatonic patterns. Each 2-bar phrase should be performed in one breath. Keep your ribs open as you sing to gain maximum control, especially on the ascending lines.

Sing this exercise two times through.

TIPS

- If necessary, work on this exercise at a slower tempo, to ensure accuracy. As you become stronger, build up to the tempo on the recording.
- Crescendo on ascending lines; decrescendo on descending lines.

Anne and Rick Peckham

Range

Anne and Rick Peckham

R&B ♩ = 112

Hey _____ yah _____ Hey _____ yah _____

Hey _____ yah _____ Hey _____ yah _____

Oo _____

Oo _____

EXERCISE 19. ROCK PENTATONIC ARPEGGIO ("BAH, BAH, BAH")

In this exercise, develop accurate, fast articulation on a pentatonic pattern in rock style. This will help you extend your range and improve your accuracy. Each pentatonic scale pattern repeats in faster rhythmic units, beginning with the scale sung in half notes and ending with the pattern in eighth notes. Sing each phrase in one breath.

Sing this exercise five times, modulating up by whole steps.

TIPS

- Articulate the consonant "B" lightly, without pressure, especially in fast eighth-note arpeggios at the highest pitch levels.
- Extend the vowel for legato singing.

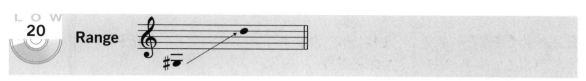

Range

Anne and Rick Peckham

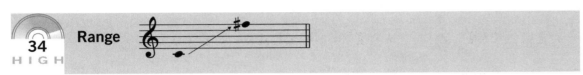

Anne and Rick Peckham

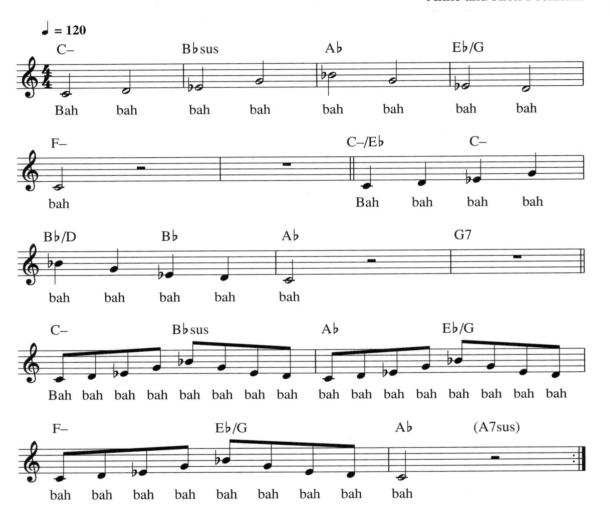

EXERCISE 20. JAZZ BALLAD ETUDE

This jazz ballad vocal study will help you develop a relaxed, free tone and efficient breath management. Sing with smooth, connected movement between notes throughout.

Sing this exercise two times through.

TIPS

- Dynamics increase gradually, peaking in bar 10, then gradually decrescendo from bar 10 to the end.
- Change vowels or create lyrics of your own.

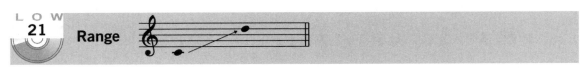

Anne and Rick Peckham

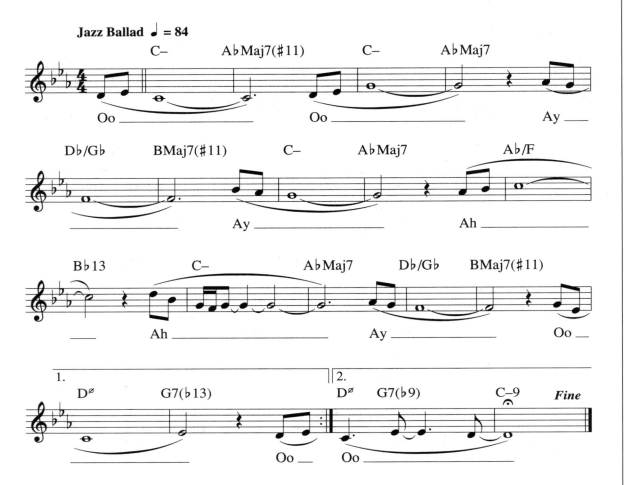

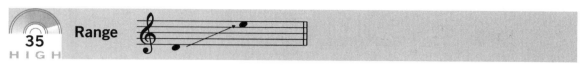

Range

35
HIGH

Anne and Rick Peckham

Singing Harmony:
Two- and Three-Part Exercises

When you first practice these exercises, begin by listening to the demonstration track with all voices, to get a feel for the style. Then work with the tracks by omitting each voice.

In the two-part exercises, the top voice is in the left channel, and the bottom voice is in the right channel. Play the track with both voices featured to learn either part you like. Then use your balance control to eliminate the part you have learned, and sing along in harmony with the other part. For example, if you choose to sing the top part in track 36, you can sing along with both voices until you feel secure with the notes and rhythms. Then use your balance control to eliminate the part you have learned, to see if you can sing your part in harmony with the other voice. Challenge yourself to try to sing each of the different parts, one after the other.

To separate the three voices for individual study in the three-part exercises, there are two tracks of each exercise. In the first track of the exercise, the top voice is in the left channel, the bottom voice is in the right channel, and the middle voice is in both. To eliminate the top voice, adjust your balance to the right. To eliminate the bottom voice, adjust your balance to the left. To hear the top and bottom without the middle voice, go to the next track. Learn one part, then work to maintain your vocal line with the other voices. Practice singing in tune, and develop basic skills for singing background harmonies.

EXERCISE 21. TWO-PART POP/ROCK ("WHO")

Simple lines with contrary motion challenge you to sing independently along with a harmony voice part. The top line requires attention to support so that the tone doesn't become flat as the line descends. The bottom part contains some harmonic dissonances that resolve quickly. This will help you develop your ear and accuracy.

TIPS

■ The top voice part is in the left channel, and the bottom voice part is in the right channel. Use your balance control to eliminate one part, so that you can sing along in harmony with the other.

■ You can choose to sing either part, or play the track several times and learn both vocal parts.

■ Take a breath every two bars.

Who

Anne Peckham

EXERCISE 22. TWO-PART R&B/POP ("GOT TO BELIEVE")

Develop your vocal skills tuning in thirds with another voice. The articulation of quick rhythmic patterns alternated with longer patterns will challenge you to sing musically, with variety in phrasing and dynamics.

TIPS

- Build dynamics in the last four bars, peaking at the last bar.
- Improvise some riffs in the last bar of the second ending, for fun.

Got to Believe

Anne Peckham

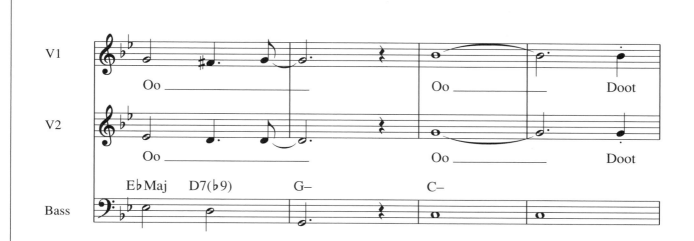

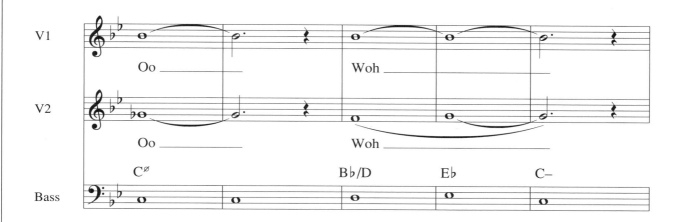

EXERCISE 23. TWO-PART FUNK ("TAKE A BREAK")

Develop rhythmic agility in this exercise. You will have to enter quickly and accurately for short bursts of harmony in thirds. In the bridge section, voices sing very close harmony—a dissonant interval of a second, resolving to a third. This requires careful listening and tuning.

Listen to the singer doing a quick bit of improvisation at the end of the second repeat. Can you add other riffs or phrases that fit in this style? Experiment with a bit of improvising.

TIP

■ Count while you sing, for accurate entrances.

Take a Break

Anne and Rick Peckham

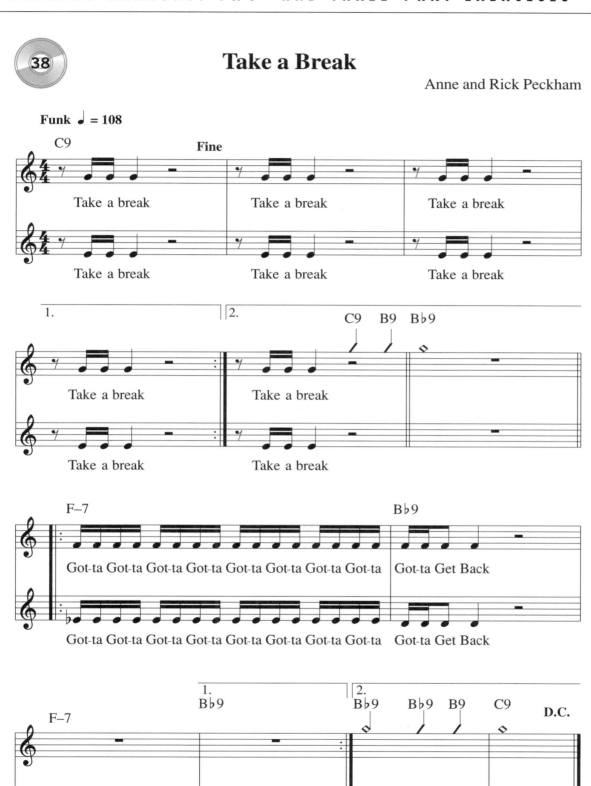

EXERCISE 24. THREE-PART COUNTRY/ROCK ("LET ME TRY")

This three-part exercise has several syncopated rhythms. Work to accent the offbeat rhythms to bring them out. The voices sing in close harmony with uniform rhythmic movement in all parts. Synchronize your entrances and cutoffs with the other voices for the cleanest sound.

The exercise is performed two times through on each track.

TIPS

■ Count rests carefully, to be sure that each entrance is accurate.

■ Use the balance control to isolate the top and bottom voices on track 39. Use track 40 to hear the exercise without the middle voice.

 All Voices   **Middle Voice Out**

Let Me Try

Anne and Rick Peckham

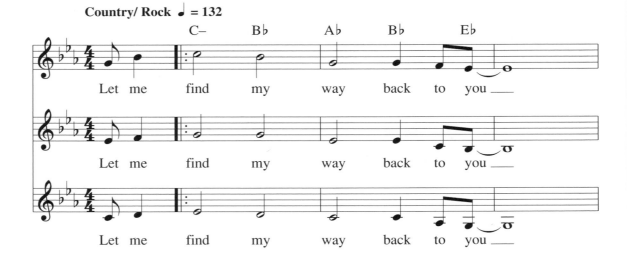

EXERCISE 25. THREE-PART ROCK ("HEY YAH")

In this exercise, work on close harmony and tuning. The voice parts require flexibility for singing the fast-moving turns. Be sure to breathe at the end of bar 4.

This exercise is performed two times through on each track.

TIPS

- After learning your own voice part, pay careful attention to the other vocal parts to be sure you are tuning accurately.
- Use track 41 to hear the example with all three voices. Use the balance control to eliminate the top or bottom voices. Use track 42 to hear the exercise with the middle voice eliminated.

41 All Voices   **42** Middle Voice Out

Hey Ya

Anne Peckham

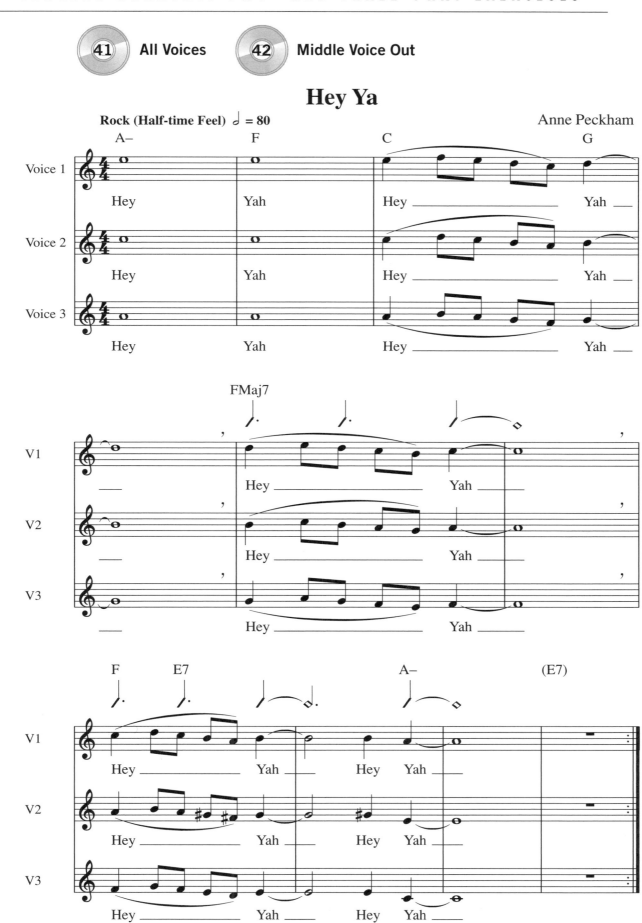

EXERCISE 26. THREE-PART BLUES ("SING FOR YOUR SUPPER")

Develop skill singing swing eighth notes on a 12-bar blues exercise. There are some tricky close harmonies between the top and middle parts. Be sure to let the intended dissonance come through. You'll also hear the performers on the recording add some expressive dynamics in bars 9 and 10. This adds musicality and style to the exercise.

This exercise is performed two times through on each track.

TIP

- Accent the syncopated rhythms at bars 3, 6, and 9.

43 All Voices   **44** Middle Voice Out

Sing for Your Supper

Anne and Rick Peckham

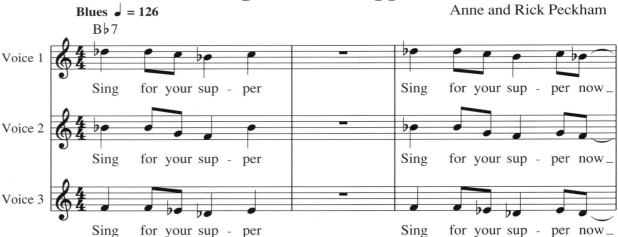

What Next?

THANK YOU for reading and singing *Vocal Workouts for the Contemporary Singer.* I hope that these techniques and exercises lead you to stronger, healthier, and more musical singing.

If you would like to learn more about vocal technique, you might find the information in my other book, *The Contemporary Singer* (Berklee Press, 2000), to be helpful in learning about the physiology of the voice and how it relates to singing technique.

To help advance your basic musicianship skills, you might also benefit from study of an instrument such as guitar or piano. Playing an instrument can help you develop confidence to learn and sing songs on your own. It also can help fuel your creative instincts and might develop your interest in writing original songs.

Look for opportunities to network with other musicians, as this will create performance opportunities. Be flexible and be resourceful.

Have a performance goal. A recording session or any kind of scheduled performance will give you a goal to work toward. Many communities have arts councils, theater groups, coffeehouses, and places of worship where musical performances are regularly scheduled. Also, look for advertisements for open mic or karaoke sessions to further your performance skills.

The *Amazing Slow Downer* and *Transkribe* are computer programs that have the capability of changing the tempo of songs without altering the pitch. They also can alter the pitch without changing the tempo of songs. You can use these programs to study fast riffs and solos of great singers. These programs provide a way for vocalists to learn directly from masterful performances. (Note that the farther you get from the original recording either in tempo or pitch, the more warbled the sound gets.) You also can slow down tempos on the workout CD of this book to study the more difficult exercises, or even change the keys to a more comfortable pitch. They also provide an easy means of looping material. Small sections from one to two bars can be repeated on a loop for more intensive study.

For more information sources and updates, please check out my Web site www.annepeckham.com. You also can find educational materials and resources at www.berkleemusic.com.

I hope that you have found this book to be useful, and I wish you the best of luck in your musical endeavors.

Photo by Susan Wilson

About the Author

NNE PECKHAM is a singer, voice teacher, and author. A professor in the Voice Department at Berklee College of Music, her work as a teacher and her publications have influenced popular singing pedagogy worldwide. Her approach embraces the foundations of good vocal technique, while building singers' skills in jazz, pop, and rock music.

At Berklee, she contributes to the voice program in many ways. In addition to teaching private voice lessons, she continues to develop curricular materials for *Elements of Vocal Technique,* a required course for all of Berklee's 600+ voice students. Her work at the college, including Berklee's Musical Theater Workshop and the Berklee Concert Choir, has helped enrich the musical experience of hundreds of students over the years. Alumni of Anne's classes and lessons include Susan Tedeschi, Juliana Hatfield, and many other professionals in the music industry.

Vocal Workouts for the Contemporary Singer is Anne's fourth publication with Berklee Press. It is the companion to *The Contemporary Singer,* a book/CD set that was recently released in a Japanese translation. She is also author of *Singer's Handbook* in the Berklee *In the Pocket* series and *Vocal Technique: Developing Your Voice for Performance,* an instructional DVD released in 2004.

A member of the National Association of Teachers of Singing, Anne served as vice president on the Boston chapter's board of directors. She has traveled extensively as a clinician and adjudicator for song and choral festivals in North America and Europe. Her master classes and vocal pedagogy seminars for students and teachers focus on approaches to rock, jazz, pop, and r&b music.

Anne sang with the Tanglewood Festival Chorus for four years, performing on two recordings with the Boston Pops, including a featured solo in their televised Gilbert and Sullivan presentation, which aired on PBS. She has performed with regional theater companies, has worked as a professional soloist with area church choirs, and performs frequently in recital and cabaret venues.